Francis Frith's
Norfolk
Living Memories

PHOTOGRAPHIC MEMORIES

Francis Frith's
Norfolk
Living Memories

Frank Meeres

FRITH
BOOK Co

First published in the United Kingdom in 2000 by
Frith Book Company Ltd

Hardback Edition 2000
ISBN 1-85937-217-1

Paperback Edition 2001
ISBN 1-85937-402-6

Reprinted in Hardback 2001
ISBN 1-85937-217-1

British Library Cataloguing in Publication Data

Francis Frith's Norfolk Living Memories
Frank Meeres

Frith Book Company Ltd
Frith's Barn, Teffont,
Salisbury, Wiltshire SP3 5QP
Tel: +44 (0) 1722 716 376
Email: info@francisfrith.co.uk
www.francisfrith.co.uk

Printed and bound in Great Britain

AS WITH ANY HISTORICAL DATABASE THE FRITH ARCHIVE IS CONSTANTLY BEING CORRECTED AND IMPROVED
AND THE PUBLISHERS WOULD WELCOME INFORMATION ON OMISSIONS OR INACCURACIES

Contents

Francis Frith: *Victorian Pioneer*

FRANCIS FRITH, Victorian founder of the world-famous photographic archive, was a complex and multi-talented man. A devout Quaker and a highly successful Victorian businessman, he was both philosophic by nature and pioneering in outlook.

By 1855 Francis Frith had already established a wholesale grocery business in Liverpool, and sold it for the astonishing sum of £200,000, which is the equivalent today of over £15,000,000. Now a multi-millionaire, he was able to indulge his passion for travel. As a child he had pored over travel books written by early explorers, and his fancy and imagination had been stirred by family holidays to the sublime mountain regions of Wales and Scotland. 'What a land of spirit-stirring and enriching scenes and places!' he had written. He was to return to these scenes of grandeur in later years to 'recapture the thousands of vivid and tender memories', but with a different purpose. Now in his thirties, and captivated by the new science of photography, Frith set out on a series of pioneering journeys to the Nile regions that occupied him from 1856 until 1860.

Intrigue and Adventure

He took with him on his travels a specially-designed wicker carriage that acted as both dark-room and sleeping chamber. These far-flung journeys were packed with intrigue and adventure. In his life story, written when he was sixty-three, Frith tells of being held captive by bandits, and of fighting 'an awful midnight battle to the very point of surrender with a deadly pack of hungry, wild dogs'. Sporting flowing Arab costume, Frith arrived at Akaba by camel seventy years before Lawrence, where he encountered 'desert princes and rival sheikhs, blazing with jewel-hilted swords'.

During these extraordinary adventures he was assiduously exploring the desert regions bordering the Nile and patiently recording the antiquities and peoples with his camera. He was the first photographer to venture beyond the sixth cataract. Africa was still the mysterious 'Dark Continent', and Stanley and Livingstone's historic meeting was a decade into the future. The conditions for picture taking confound belief. He laboured for hours in his wicker dark-room in the sweltering heat of the desert, while the volatile chemicals fizzed dangerously in their trays. Often he was forced to work in remote tombs and caves where conditions were cooler. Back in London he exhibited his photographs and was 'rapturously cheered' by members of the Royal Society. His reputation as a photographer was made overnight. An eminent modern historian has likened their impact on the population of the time to that on our own generation of the first photographs taken on the surface of the moon.

Venture of a Life-Time

Characteristically, Frith quickly spotted the opportunity to create a new business as a specialist publisher of photographs. He lived in an era of immense and sometimes violent change. For the poor in the early part of Victoria's reign work was a drudge and the hours long, and people had precious little free time to enjoy themselves. Most had no transport other than a cart or gig at their disposal, and had not travelled far beyond the boundaries of their own town or village.

However, by the 1870s, the railways had threaded their way across the country, and Bank Holidays and half-day Saturdays had been made obligatory by Act of Parliament. All of a sudden the ordinary working man and his family were able to enjoy days out and see a little more of the world.

With characteristic business acumen, Francis Frith foresaw that these new tourists would enjoy having souvenirs to commemorate their days out. In 1860 he married Mary Ann Rosling and set out with the intention of photographing every city, town and village in Britain. For the next thirty years he travelled the country by train and by pony and trap, producing fine photographs of seaside resorts and beauty spots that were keenly bought by millions of Victorians. These prints were painstakingly pasted into family albums and pored over during the dark nights of winter, rekindling precious memories of summer excursions.

The Rise of Frith & Co

Frith's studio was soon supplying retail shops all over the country. To meet the demand he gathered about him a small team of photographers, and published the work of independent artist-photographers of the calibre of Roger Fenton and Francis Bedford. In order to gain some understanding of the scale of Frith's business one only has to look at the catalogue issued by Frith & Co in 1886: it runs to some 670 pages, listing not only many thousands of views of the British Isles but also many photographs of most European countries, and China, Japan, the USA and Canada – note the sample page shown above

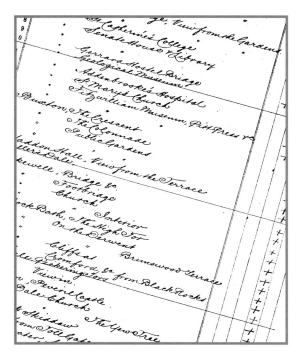

from the hand-written *Frith & Co* ledgers detailing pictures taken. By 1890 Frith had created the greatest specialist photographic publishing company in the world, with over 2,000 outlets – more than the combined number that Boots and WH Smith have today! The picture on the right shows the *Frith & Co* display board at Ingleton in the Yorkshire Dales. Beautifully constructed with mahogany frame and gilt inserts, it could display up to a dozen local scenes.

Postcard Bonanza

The ever-popular holiday postcard we know today took many years to develop. In 1870 the Post Office issued the first plain cards, with a pre-printed stamp on one face. In 1894 they allowed other publishers' cards to be sent through the mail with an attached adhesive halfpenny stamp. Demand grew rapidly, and in 1895 a new size of postcard was permitted

called the court card, but there was little room for illustration. In 1899, a year after Frith's death, a new card measuring 5.5 x 3.5 inches became the standard format, but it was not until 1902 that the divided back came into being, with address and message on one face and a full-size illustration on the other. *Frith & Co* were in the vanguard of postcard development, and Frith's sons Eustace and Cyril continued their father's monumental task, expanding the number of views offered to the public and recording more and more places in Britain, as the coasts and countryside were opened up to mass travel.

Francis Frith died in 1898 at his villa in Cannes, his great project still growing. The archive he created continued in business for another seventy years. By 1970 it contained over a third of a million pictures of 7,000 cities, towns and villages. The massive photographic record Frith has left to us stands as a living monument to a special and very remarkable man.

Frith's Archive: *A Unique Legacy*

FRANCIS FRITH'S legacy to us today is of immense significance and value, for the magnificent archive of evocative photographs he created provides a unique record of change in 7,000 cities, towns and villages throughout Britain over a century and more. Frith and his fellow studio photographers revisited locations many times down the years to update their views, compiling for us an enthralling and colourful pageant of British life and character.

We tend to think of Frith's sepia views of Britain as nostalgic, for most of us use them to conjure up memories of places in our own lives with which we have family associations. It often makes us forget that to Francis Frith they were records of daily life as it was actually being lived in the cities, towns and villages of his day. The Victorian age was one of great and often bewildering change for ordinary people, and though the pictures evoke an impression of slower times, life was as busy and hectic as it is today.

We are fortunate that Frith was a photographer of the people, dedicated to recording the minutiae of everyday life. For it is this sheer wealth of visual data, the painstaking chronicle of changes in dress, transport, street layouts, buildings, housing, engineering and landscape that captivates us so much today. His remarkable images offer us a powerful link with the past and with the lives of our ancestors.

Today's Technology

Computers have now made it possible for Frith's many thousands of images to be accessed almost instantly. In the Frith archive today, each photograph is carefully 'digitised' then stored on a CD Rom. Frith archivists can locate a single photograph amongst thousands within seconds. Views can be catalogued and sorted under a variety of categories of place and content to the immediate benefit of researchers.

Inexpensive reference prints can be created for them at the touch of a mouse button, and a wide range of books and other printed materials assembled and published for a wider, more general readership - in the next twelve months over a hundred Frith local history titles will be published! The day-to-day workings of the archive are very different from how they were in Francis Frith's time: imagine the herculean task of sorting through eleven tons of glass negatives as Frith had to do to locate a

See Frith at www.francisfrith.co.uk

particular sequence of pictures! Yet the archive still prides itself on maintaining the same high standards of excellence laid down by Francis Frith, including the painstaking cataloguing and indexing of every view.

It is curious to reflect on how the internet now allows researchers in America and elsewhere greater instant access to the archive than Frith himself ever enjoyed. Many thousands of individual views can be called up on screen within seconds on one of the Frith internet sites, enabling people living continents away to revisit the streets of their ancestral home town, or view places in Britain where they have enjoyed holidays. Many overseas researchers welcome the chance to view special theme selections, such as transport, sports, costume and ancient monuments.

We are certain that Francis Frith would have heartily approved of these modern developments in imaging techniques, for he himself was always working at the very limits of Victorian photographic technology.

The Value of the Archive Today

Because of the benefits brought by the computer, Frith's images are increasingly studied by social historians, by researchers into genealogy and ancestory, by architects, town planners, and by teachers and schoolchildren involved in local history projects.

In addition, the archive offers every one of us an opportunity to examine the places where we and our families have lived and worked down the years. Highly successful in Frith's own era, the archive is now, a century and more on, entering a new phase of popularity.

The Past in Tune with the Future

Historians consider the Francis Frith Collection to be of prime national importance. It is the only archive of its kind remaining in private ownership and has been valued at a million pounds. However, this figure is now rapidly increasing as digital technology enables more and more people around the world to enjoy its benefits.

Francis Frith's archive is now housed in an historic timber barn in the beautiful village of Teffont in Wiltshire. Its founder would not recognize the archive office as it is today. In place of the many thousands of dusty boxes containing glass plate negatives and an all-pervading odour of photographic chemicals, there are now ranks of computer screens. He would be amazed to watch his images travelling round the world at unimaginable speeds through network and internet lines.

The archive's future is both bright and exciting. Francis Frith, with his unshakeable belief in making photographs available to the greatest number of people, would undoubtedly approve of what is being done today with his lifetime's work. His photographs, depicting our shared past, are now bringing pleasure and enlightenment to millions around the world a century and more after his death.

NORFOLK LIVING MEMORIES
An Introduction

'VERY FLAT, NORFOLK', wrote Noel Coward, and this is the opinion of many people who have not been to the county. However, although Norfolk is admittedly flat in parts, especially in the extreme west and east, the main part is far from flat, with rolling hills, a ridge of high land running south-north in the west of the county, and some very respectable cliffs.

At one time Norfolk was indeed flat: almost eighty million years ago it was at the bottom of the North Sea. It was then that the chalk beds were laid down, containing nodules of silicon - flints, in other words. As land and sea levels slowly altered, the chalk bed tilted; it is exposed in west Norfolk, but in the east the chalk has become overlaid by later sedimentary rocks.

This ancient history explains a key element of Norfolk today: its building materials. For most of the county the traditional building material is flint, an exceptionally hard material. This can be used as whole flints, with their white surface, or the flints can be cut in half, producing a very dark appearance. They can even be cut into little squares and used to infill limestone or chalk to create delicate patterns known as flushwork. However, in the villages of west Norfolk carstone beneath the chalk comes to the surface; this, a distinctive orange-brown stone, is the main building material.

Ancient men recognised the value of flint not as a building material, but for axes. They mined it 6,000 years ago, and their mines can still be seen at Grimes' Graves. Thus, from the beginning Norfolk has been an industrial area, and a

relatively well-populated and wealthy one - finds of Iron Age treasures have included the fabulous horde of gold necklaces discovered at Snettisham.

Written history begins with the Romans: one of Norfolk's earliest-named residents is also one of the most famous - Boudicca, Queen of the Iceni, whose rebellion was such a threat to the Roman invaders. The Romans responded by building a town at Caistor, south of Norwich, to impose order. As the threat of invasion by the Saxons from across the North Sea grew, the Romans built forts along the coast at Burgh Castle, Caister by Yarmouth and Brancaster. However, at the beginning of the 5th century the Romans departed, and there was no-one to stop the Saxon invasions. Gradually these people settled and established the Saxon kingdom of East Anglia, probably centred round Sutton Hoo in Suffolk where their kings were buried.

After the Saxons came the Scandinavians or Vikings, at first raiding and then settling. Although the area was only briefly under Viking rule (from 870 to 914), their influence is strong, not so much in buildings as in place-names. After the Vikings came the Normans, second-generation Vikings themselves, defeating the English - as everyone knows - at the Battle of Hastings in 1066. They were builders of great castles and great churches, many of which are still key elements in the Norfolk landscape.

Domesday Book, compiled in 1086, shows East Anglia to be the richest and most densely-populated part of England at this time, and it remained so throughout the Middle Ages. This wealth was based on wool. The woollen trade made Norwich the largest city in England (apart from London); the county also boasted two of the busiest ports in the country, Yarmouth serving Norwich, and Lynn serving many towns of eastern England through the extensive waterways that reach the sea at the Wash. The ports of the north coast - Blakeney, Wells, Cley and others - were important too, trading with Europe and as far away as Iceland. Another source of wealth was fish, a vital part of the diet of the Middle Ages when meat was scarce and could not in any case be eaten during Lent or the many holy days of the Christian year.

Because Norfolk was so heavily populated, its most characteristic features - the Broads and the Fens - are man-made landscapes. The Broads are in fact pits caused by digging out peat for fuel to supply the hearths of Norwich and elsewhere. As these pits were dug, water levels were slowly rising: in the end the pits were flooded to become inland lakes. In the Fens, man's work had the opposite result. The Fens were once under water, either permanently or during wet seasons and high tides. The process of draining these areas has been going on since Roman times; the single time of greatest effort was the 1640s under the

Dutch engineer Cornelius Vermuyden. In the east, the whole area beyond Acle was originally under water too - in Roman times this was a vast shallow estuary bounded by Caister to the north and Burgh to the south. Gradually a sandbank emerged, which was immediately occupied by fishermen: from these beginnings grew the town of Great Yarmouth. Continual drainage has turned the marshes into farmland. Two hundred years ago the main road from Yarmouth to Norwich ran well to the north, keeping to the low hills. It was only in 1828 that the marshes had been drained sufficiently for the Acle Straight to be built, creating a direct road route between the two towns.

Thus the most important transport links were by water. Goods from Europe were offloaded at Yarmouth and put onto wherries, the flat-bottomed, broad-beamed boats with black sails that are seen in so many pictures of Norfolk life. The main trade was, of course, up the Yare to Norwich, but the other rivers - the Bure, the Ant and the Thurne - were busy too. Where the rivers were too shallow, they began to be canalised: this allowed wherries to travel further upstream, to Aylsham and to North Walsham. The same process applied in the west of the county, where the Little Ouse was similarly treated to allow access to Thetford by barges.

Drainage in both the Fens and the Broads has had an important effect on the landscape - the rivers running through the areas are much higher than the land, which is protected from flooding only by the river banks. Excess water from the low-lying land has to be got rid of by being pumped up into the rivers. This is the purpose of the drainage mill. Those of the Fens have almost all gone, and have been largely replaced by more powerful engines. However, mills are still a key element in the Broadland landscape: the brick towers of over 70 drainage mills still stand, although only a very few now have their sails.

Norfolk has a very varied landscape for such a relatively small area. Another distinctive region lies to the south-west, where the soil is so sandy that it could only be farmed in brecks - areas of land cultivated for a year or two and then allowed to revert to nature. This was great rabbit country - warrens were common throughout the area, at Thetford, Methwold and elsewhere.

Norfolk's importance in the wool trade declined in the late 18th century as watermills in Yorkshire and Lancashire harnessed the power of fast-flowing streams: there were a few watermills in Norfolk, but the slow-moving streams were far from ideal. Norfolk's decline was only a relative one: it remained a prosperous farming area, the heart of the late 18th-century Agricultural Revolution. Industries based on agriculture were booming too, including brewing. By the later 18th and early 19th century, Norwich dominated

the brewing industry of the region. The many smaller breweries were taken over to form four giant concerns: Bullard, Morgan, Youngs and Steward & Patteson. These continued into the 1960s, when Watney Mann swallowed up all four. The only major brewery in Norfolk outside Norwich was Lacon's at Yarmouth. This owned a large number of public houses in east Norfolk: it was eventually taken over by Whitbread.

The most dramatic of the attempts to improve navigation came too late. This was the New Cut, a long straight channel through the marshes, which was intended to allow ocean-going ships direct access to Norwich by by-passing the shallow reaches of Breydon Water. A massive harbour was planned at Norwich, but the scheme was abandoned: the railway had arrived.

The first railway in Norfolk ran from Yarmouth to Norwich, opening in 1844. Soon this connected the area with London and the Midlands, and over the next 50 years the railway reached every town in Norfolk and many villages too - at the peak of the railway age there were over 150 stations in the county. The effects were revolutionary: soon the train was taking Norfolk products, such as turkeys and herrings, to London. Railways worked the other way too, opening up Norfolk to visitors from the cities, and thus developing the holiday trade on which the county has increasingly come to depend.

Norfolk had begun to attract tourists in a small way when sea-bathing became fashionable in the mid 18th century - Yarmouth opened its first Bath House on the sea front in 1759. Cromer was mentioned by Jane Austen in 'Emma': one of her characters calls it 'the best of all the sea-bathing places'. Once the railway connected Yarmouth and Norwich, day-trips from the city to the seaside very soon became popular.

As the railway expanded in the later 19th century, so did the tourist trade, especially along the east coast. This area became very much the home of the holiday camp. The first appears to have been that set up at Caister in 1906 by Socialists seeking a break from their labours among the poor in London. This was followed by many others, including the 'big two' - Pontin's and Butlin's. Between the wars, chalets and caravan sites began to appear among the sand dunes behind the beach all along the coast. Parts of the north coast were developing too - the resort at Hunstanton was deliberately planned by the local landowners, the L'Estrange family of Hunstanton Hall. The north-east coast was popularised by a Londoner named Clement Scott, who loved Overstrand and coined a new name for this part of Norfolk: 'Poppyland'. The railway came here as well, giving direct access from London and from the Midlands.

The Broads, too, could be said to owe their origins as a holiday area to one man, George Christopher Davies, whose books praised the

delights of boating holidays. The first boats for hire were wherries, often ones no longer needed for carrying goods. Early in the century came steam boats, followed by internal combustion engines. By 1949 there were 547 boats for hire on the Broads, of which 301 were motor boats. The area was further popularised by Arthur Ransome in his classic children's books 'Coot Club' and 'The Big Six' written in the 1930s. Over-expansion of the holiday trade has caused problems in some areas: the Broads have lost the crystal-clear water that was once one of their most-prized characteristics. The greatest attraction of the Broads was, of course, the wildlife, especially the birds. As appreciation of nature has grown, so the previously rather neglected north coast has become popular too:

its marshes are a paradise for bird lovers and walkers.

Norfolk in the 20th century has seen growth, but it has seen decline too. Many of the small towns and villages are less populated than they were a century ago: the mechanisation of agriculture has led to an enormous loss of jobs in farming areas. Villages have gradually lost many of their key elements - the railway station, the local bus, the school, the post office and general stores, the inn. These photographs capture Norfolk at a time when tourism and village life were both flourishing: some of the pictures taken half a century ago already seem to reflect a style of life light-years away from the Norfolk of the new millennium.

Broadland

THE BROADS c1945 T213330
Here we see a peaceful scene on the upper reaches of the
river Bure. There are reed-beds along the far side of the river.
Boats have been available for hire in Broadland since at least
the 1880s, and motor launches first became available in the
years following the First World War.

HORSTEAD, THE OLD MILL c1960 H343012

HORSTEAD
The Old Mill c1960

This mill, on the river Bure, was the largest of the watermills in Norfolk. Because of the flat terrain, this was an undershot mill - the stream turned the wheel by passing underneath it, rather than flowing over it. The mill was destroyed by fire in 1963: only the millpond and a few brick arches now survive.

◆

COLTISHALL
At the Locks c1955

Coltishall was a prosperous town in the 18th and 19th centuries, when trade was carried by river rather than the road. It had malthouses and shipbuilding yards: the last trading wherry on the Broads was built in the Anchor Street boatyard here in 1912.

COLTISHALL, AT THE LOCKS c1955 C417007

COLTISHALL
The Old Lock c1955

Coltishall was the natural limit of navigation up the river Bure. In 1779 the navigable river was extended a further ten miles to Aylsham by means of a series of locks. These were built wider than normal canal locks in order to take wherries, which were broader in the beam than ordinary barges.

COLTISHALL
The Village c1965

This is the open space that makes up the centre of Coltishall. Summer trade is served by the Eldorado ice cream cart with its well-known invitation to 'Stop Me'. Coltishall is one of several Norfolk villages said to be haunted by Old Shuck - a black dog the size of a calf.

COLTISHALL, THE OLD LOCK c1955 C417037

COLTISHALL, THE VILLAGE c1955 C417027

HOVETON
THE VILLAGE c1955 H399137
Hoveton is one of the centres of Broadland, and is crowded in the summer months. Roy's family store has grown out of a grocer's shop started at the beginning of the 20th century to cater for the needs of 'Yachting and Boating Parties'. By the time of this photograph, it had expanded to take over almost all the buildings in the town centre.

HORNING, THE FERRY INN c1960 H116116

A chain ferry used to cross the river Bure at this point, similar to that still operating at Reedham Ferry. Horning is one of the prettiest villages in Broadland: almost all the houses along the river have waterways and boathouses of their own.

LUDHAM, POST OFFICE CORNER c1955 L110075

The Post Office boasts a range of enamel advertising signs. Behind it is the parish church of St Catherine with its large flint tower. The church contains a beautiful rood screen and a rare medieval painting of the Crucifixion.

LUDHAM, THE VILLAGE C1955 L110119
Old cottages, some with roofs thatched with Norfolk reed, line the main road opposite Ludham churchyard: the Celtic-style cross on the left is the War Memorial. The poet William Cowper was brought up in Ludham Hall.

RANWORTH, THE BROAD C1960 R9047
The reed-beds on the right of the picture have been cut, and the reeds will be used for thatching roofs. The boy in the small boat is quanting, a word used on the Broads for propelling a boat by means of a long pole.

ACLE, THE MOORING c1960 A204057

Looking eastwards along the river Bure, this photograph shows a wide range of sailing and motor boats. The name 'Lavengro' is the title of a book by George Borrow, the Victorian writer and linguist: he was born at East Dereham in Norfolk.

ACLE, THE BRIDGE HOTEL FROM THE BRIDGE c1955 A204068

The hotel is on the site of the medieval monastery of Weybridge, a small house of canons providing hospitality for travellers between Great Yarmouth and Norwich, both by road and by river. The hotel is continuing the same tradition - however, monasteries did not charge for their hospitality!

ACLE, THE VILLAGE C1955 A204084
Acle lies exactly halfway between Great Yarmouth and Norwich. The church is dedicated to St Edmund: it has a thatched nave roof and an octagonal top to its round tower. It contains a rare inscription describing the devastating effects of a plague in the Middle Ages.

STOKESBY, THE FERRY INN C1955 S469014
Many of the inns along the broads contain the word 'Ferry', commemorating long-gone crossing points. The ferries were often run by the innkeepers themselves, who benefited from the extra trade. Stokesby has two windmills, one for corn and the other for drainage.

STOKESBY, THE VILLAGE C1965 S469047

STOKESBY
The Village c1965
An enormous horse-chestnut tree dominates this photograph of a typical Broadland village: reed cutting is still carried out here. This area of Norfolk is sheep country, and Stokesby is mentioned in the Domesday Book of 1086 as having 180 sheep in the manorial flock.

STALHAM
The Staithe c1955
Stalham was a minor port in the 19th century, as the warehouse buildings in this picture show. In front are two Norfolk wherries: the black sail that can be seen on the further boat is a characteristic of these broad-beamed, shallow-bottomed craft.

STALHAM, THE STAITHE C1955 S467045

STALHAM, THE ENTRANCE TO CANAL c1955 S467069

STALHAM
The Entrance to Canal c1955
19th-century cottages are reflected in the water on a still day. The North Walsham and Dilham canal begins beyond the bridge, which is called Wayford Bridge. The name comes from the Saxon word for 'road', which suggests that there has been a river crossing here for over a thousand years.

SUTTON
The Windmill c1955
This corn windmill is reputed to be the tallest in Norfolk, nine floors high. The boat-shaped cap is characteristic of Norfolk mills. The mill was built in 1859, replacing an earlier one that had been destroyed by fire. Since 1976 it has been restored, and is now open to the public.

SUTTON, THE WINDMILL c1955 S473016

POTTER HEIGHAM
The Bridge c1926
This is one of the very few medieval bridges surviving on the Broadland rivers. It is supposedly haunted by a phantom coach and four, which is driven by the Devil, dressed as a Bishop: it appears at midnight and plunges from the bridge into the water below.

◆

POTTER HEIGHAM
Near the Bridge c1926
The bridge at Potter Heigham has headroom of only six feet at high tide. This has meant an active time for generations of sailors - sails and masts have to be lowered to pass under the bridge and raised again on the other side.

POTTER HEIGHAM, THE BRIDGE c1926 P167041

POTTER HEIGHAM, NEAR THE BRIDGE c1926 P167024

POTTER HEIGHAM, THE REGATTA c1955 P167018

The Broads attract not just holidaymakers hiring cruisers on a weekly basis, but also serious sailors, and annual regattas bring thousands of boats of all sizes to the villages. Early regattas were known as Water Frolics: Norwich Castle Museum has an enormous painting of the Thorpe Water Frolic of 1824 by local artist Joseph Stannard.

POTTER HEIGHAM, ON THE THURNE c1926 P167040

Chalets and holiday homes have lined parts of the river Thurne since the 1920s. Behind is High's drainage mill, still complete with sails and with a fantail to turn the cap so that the sails are taking up the wind.

MARTHAM, THE POND C1955 M228019

Martham is one of the prettiest villages of east Norfolk, with its large green and village pond. Martham church contains a memorial erected by Mr Christopher Burraway to 'Alice, who by her life was my Sister, my Mistress, my Mother and my Wife'. No-one knows its exact meaning!

HICKLING, THE STAITHE FROM THE PLEASURE BOAT INN C1955 H307049

'Staithe' is an Anglo-Saxon word for landing-place. It is the word used for all mooring places on the Broads, whether along the river or up an inlet. Beyond the staithe, the inlet opens into Hickling Broad, which at 400 acres is the largest of the Norfolk Broads.

THORPE ST ANDREW
High Street c1955 T250002

Thorpe is two miles east of Norwich; it became a popular
spot for Sunday outings from the mid 19th century, despite
the disapproval of some church authorities in the city.
Many villages have road bypasses, but Thorpe has a river
bypass: through traffic uses a stretch of river created by the
railway builders in 1844, and only leisure traffic calls here.
The present church of St Andrew replaced the medieval
one in the 1860s: the tower, here seen under repair, is 150
feet high. Thorpe Green lies to the left of the picture: a
boat can be seen on the river through the trees. The
painter John Sell Cotman was born in Thorpe.

BRUNDALL
The River Stores c1955 B497014
Shops along the river Yare serve the needs
of boating holidaymakers along this
beautiful stretch of the river, four miles
downstream from Norwich. Brundall parish
church has an unusual feature: it contains
the only lead font in Norfolk.

CANTLEY, THE RED HOUSE HOTEL c1965 C414005
The hotel is on ground well below the level of the water in the river Yare, and is protected from flooding by the riverbank. Excess water has to be pumped up from the low-lying land and discharged along the rivers: this is now done by electric pump.

REEDHAM, THE FERRY c1955 R303061
The chain-ferry at Reedham is one of the last survivals of its kind: it is a raft hauled across the river by means of a wheel pulling on a chain. When not being used by the ferry, the chain is at the bottom of the river. This is the southern bank of the river Yare, which is in open country.

REEDHAM
The Ferry Inn c1955 R303068
This is one of the most popular of the Broadland river inns, equally
accessible by road or river. Note the chain of coloured light-bulbs
along the front: at night this inn could be seen from several miles
away down the river.

The East Coast

BRADWELL
The Sun Inn c1955 B496003
The village inn was owned by Steward and Patteson, one of the
four large breweries of Norwich. Bradwell is one of a group of
villages just south of Great Yarmouth which were in Suffolk
until boundary changes of 1974 brought them into Norfolk.

BRADWELL, THE CHURCH c1955 B496004

This is an excellent example of an East Anglian round tower. No one is sure if they are round because of the difficulty of making corners out of flint, or because they were built for defensive purposes, or because the builders simply liked the look of round towers.

GORLESTON, BRUSH QUAY c1955 G35009
Gorleston developed as a fishing port and rival to Yarmouth across the estuary of the river Yare. It became part of Great Yarmouth in the early 19th century. This scene is dominated by the lighthouse, built in 1887.

GREAT YARMOUTH, BRITANNIA PIER c1955 G56015
The Royal Aquarium, to the left, was built in 1875 to house a skating rink and aquarium: it later became a cinema. The Britannia Pier has had a exciting life, having been burnt down at least three times, once by suffragettes. In front of the pier is a 'Noah's Ark' fun ride.

GREAT YARMOUTH, THE BATHING POOL AND THE JETTY c1955 G56041
The jetty has played an important part in English history, as it was from here that Admiral Nelson set out to join his fleet and fight many of his most famous battles. The bathing pool seen here has been recently restored after suffering damage in the disastrous floods of 1953.

GREAT YARMOUTH, PONY RIDES c1955 G56030
Pony rides have always been popular in Yarmouth; the problem of disposal of the droppings is still a disputed one, with local authorities sometimes suggesting that the ponies should wear nappies. The large building behind was originally the Gem, the first cinema in Norfolk; in its early years the authorities insisted that men and women sit in separate parts of the auditorium.

CAISTER-ON-SEA, THE 'CAMP SPECIAL' ARRIVING AT CAISTER HOLIDAY CAMP c1955 C450004
The 'Holiday Camps Express' ran from London to Caister and the other Norfolk holiday camps at California, Scratby and Hemsby every Saturday in summer from 1934 to 1938, and again from 1948 to 1958. The new arrivals all look very happy!

CAISTER-ON-SEA
The Life Boat c1955 C450112
This is the 'Jose Neville', the first motor lifeboat to be used at Caister: she came into service in 1941. She is the direct descendant of the 'Beauchamp', lost in the lifeboat disaster of 1901 when nine local lifeboatmen drowned as the boat capsized. There is a memorial to them in Caister cemetery.

CAISTER-ON-SEA, PLEASURE FLIGHTS OVER GREAT YARMOUTH c1955 C450300
The air age came to Yarmouth as early as 1913, when an Air Station was established on the South Denes. Caister itself was the scene of an early experiment in the postal service: in the summer of 1948, a daily helicopter flew from here to Peterborough carrying mail. The scheme only lasted for a few months.

CALIFORNIA, THE CALIFORNIA INN c1960 C413011
Norfolk's own California is just north of Caister. The 'Cali' has satisfied the thirst of generations of holidaymakers, but before the tourists came it served the community of beachmen who lived here from 1850 onwards. They were salvagemen, and earned their living from the many wrecks along this coast.

SCRATBY, THE STEPS c1955 S463034

The sand-dunes along the east coast of Norfolk can rise to heights of ten metres or more, making access to the beautiful sandy beaches relatively difficult. The east coast has always been open to the threat of enemy invasion, as the concrete pill-box further along the cliff indicates.

SCRATBY, GENERAL VIEW c1955 S463036

These superior chalets are on the sand-dunes above the beach; as estates like this are privately-owned, the roads are usually not made up. The chalets further up the road are on the cliff top, and are extremely vulnerable to coastal erosion.

HEMSBY, THE VILLAGE c1955 H306300
There are several villages in east Norfolk whose names end in '-by': this indicates that they were originally founded by the Vikings. Most of them are in the area known as Flegg, itself a Viking word for a marshy place.

NEWPORT, THE LACON ARMS c1955 N137060
The Lacons were a brewing family with a brewery in Great Yarmouth; they also owned a large estate in the Ormesby and Hemsby area. The brewery was taken over by Whitbread in 1965 and stopped brewing just three years later.

NEWPORT, THE VALLEY c1960 N137070

Newport was founded by a group of beachmen or salvagers in 1841; nine of the founders were drowned attempting a salvage operation in the following year. The 1950s saw a rapid development of holiday chalets among the sand-dunes between Hemsby village and the sea.

WINTERTON-ON-SEA, THE LANE c1955 W357034

The inn is named the Fisherman's Return. Winterton Ness was one of the most dangerous points along the English coast, and many ships have been lost here. Daniel Defoe describes a single night in 1692 when over 200 ships and a thousand lives were lost in a terrible storm.

WINTERTON-ON-SEA, THE BEACH ROAD c1955 W357036
The unmade road leads from the village to the beach. The sand-dunes are covered with marram grass, which helps knit them together and prevent erosion on this windy coast. The church here, as in many coastal parishes, has a very tall tower to act as a landmark: Winterton church tower is 130 feet high.

WINTERTON-ON-SEA
The Beach Road c1955 W357077
This photograph shows the village end of the Beach Road, with two general stores, both carrying many advertisement signs. More spiritual needs are catered for by the Methodist chapel on the right, built in 1876. The sea is just beyond the dunes in the distance.

North-East Norfolk

SEA PALLING
THE VILLAGE C1955 S470013
Here we see the 19th-century cottages of the village; the older part is well inland, and the newer development stretches from the old centre towards the sea. The sea is still approached through a gap in the dunes known as the Cart Gap, a reflection of an age when the sea and the coast were for business rather than for pleasure.

HAPPISBURGH, CHURCH FARM c1965 H304067
The farm and its outbuildings, roofed with Norfolk thatch, date from the 18th century. The church beyond is dedicated to St Mary. The tower is 110 feet high and, because of its prominent position, it was bombed in the Second World War. It was repaired in 1956-8.

WALCOTT, THE OLD MANOR HOUSE c1955 W400018
The thatched roof of Norfolk reed covers the main house and the outbuildings in one enormous sweep, reaching almost to the ground. Sir Samuel Bignold, the man who made the Norwich Union a great insurance company, was lord of the manor here, but he did not live in the house.

WALCOTT
The Beech Bough Hotel c1965

Hotels and bed and breakfast accommodation make up a key element in the tourist economy of Norfolk, especially in Yarmouth and the other resorts of the east coast. The beech tree after which the hotel is named has long disappeared.

WALCOTT
The Lighthouse Inn c1955

There is no evidence of a lighthouse here, so the inn is presumably named for the lighthouse at nearby Happisburgh, with its distinctive red and white stripes, built in 1791. Its lantern is 136 feet above the water.

WALCOTT, THE BEECH BOUGH HOTEL C1965 W400052

WALCOTT, THE LIGHTHOUSE INN C1955 W400011

BACTON, SCOTTS ESTATE c1955 B493044
The spread of the holiday industry along the north-east Norfolk coast is reflected in this mixture of mobile caravans and fixed chalets. Bacton is now also the place where gas from the Norfolk Sea fields is brought ashore.

BACTON, THE KING'S ARMS c1955 B493068
Bacton was an important village in medieval Norfolk, because its monastery (at Bromholme) was one of the most-visited places of pilgrimage in England: it possessed a section of the True Cross, a very holy relic mentioned both by Chaucer and in 'Piers Ploughman'.

TRIMINGHAM, CHURCH STREET c1955 T226011
Village shop and parish church form the heart of this cliff-top village. Walls and houses are built of whole flints. The tree bending towards the church reflects the wind-swept character of this isolated corner of Norfolk. A tourist guidebook claims that the towers of no less than 50 churches can be seen from the highest point in the parish.

CAWSTON, HIGH STREET c1965 C415007
The Dutch gables on the houses along both sides of this street are a good example of the influence that the many Dutch and Flemish immigrants to Norfolk from the 16th century onwards have had over local life: their most famous import is the canary, from which Norwich City football club take their colours and their nickname.

REEPHAM, FROM THE CHURCH TOWER c1965 R304007
The tower from which this photograph was taken belongs to one of three churches that occupied a single churchyard. In Norfolk it is relatively common to find two churches in one churchyard, and occasionally, as here, three: the reason for this is not clearly understood.

REEPHAM, MARKET PLACE c1965 R304023

The long white house opposite was originally the home of Reepham Brewery, quite a large concern with over 50 public houses. Like almost all local breweries in the county, it was taken over by one of the big four breweries of Norwich, in this case by Bullard's in 1878.

BOOTON, THE MAIN STREET c1965 B539002

Booton is a small village in North Norfolk, known mainly for its beautiful Victorian church built at his own expense and to his own design by the rector, Whitwell Elwin, who served the church for 50 years: he died in 1900 aged 83.

AYLSHAM, RED LION LANE c1955 A220002

Here we see the narrow main street of this north Norfolk market town. The road sign on the left depicts a torch, and warns of a school just around the corner. The slate-hung gable on the building to the left is unusual for Norfolk.

AYLSHAM, THE MARKET PLACE AND THE HOTEL c1965 A220026

The 18th-century coaching inn, the Black Boys, with its Dutch gable, is in the centre of the picture. Aylsham Market Place is part of the estate of Blickling Hall, two miles to the west, which was at one time owned by the Boleyn family. Like the Hall itself, the Market Place is now owned by the National Trust.

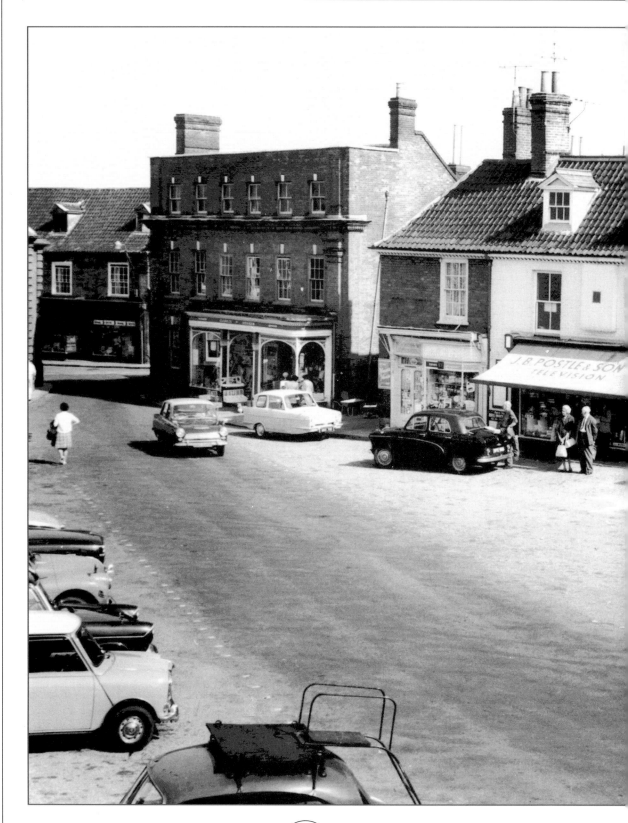

AYLSHAM
MARKET PLACE c1965 A220047
A market town like Aylsham supplies a wide range of services to customers in the town and in surrounding villages: here these include greetings cards, a printing service and the supply and repair of televisions.

ALDBOROUGH, THE BLACK BOYS c1955 A278003
Shop and inn make up the heart of this village, built round the edge of an enormous village green. There was a market here from at least 1280. The Black Boys is owned by Morgan and Co, another of the four great breweries of Norwich.

WORSTEAD, THE WEAVER'S COTTAGE c1955 W355010
As the name of this cottage suggests, Worstead was one of the main centres of the weaving industry, which made Norfolk one of the wealthiest regions of medieval England. Weavers' money paid for the building of the grand parish church, one of the largest in Norfolk.

BRADFIELD, THE VILLAGE c1955 B321010

Small houses are built along the village street, many with their bedrooms formed in the roof-space. The houses are straight on to the road, with no front gardens: however, they have long gardens at the rear. Bradfield church tower took over 50 years to build; from its summit it is possible to see twelve other churches.

NORTH WALSHAM, MARKET PLACE c1955 N42020

The spectacular Market Cross was built in about 1600, replacing one burnt down in the major town fire of that year. Paston Free School is close to the Market Place: former pupils include Horatio Nelson and H Rider Haggard, author of 'King Solomon's Mines'.

NORTH WALSHAM, BACTONWOOD MILL, SPA COMMON c1955 N42007
This mill is the best-preserved of the Norfolk watermills, with all its machinery still surviving. The mill is on the North Walsham and Dilham Canal. Sir William Cubitt, an engineer best known for inventing the prison treadmill, was born here in 1785.

THORPE MARKET, THE GREEN c1955 T256006
Traditional Norfolk cottages with thatched roofs and flint walls are built on the edge of a large village green: this kind of green-edge or common-edge settlement is characteristic of Norfolk. As its name suggests, this tiny village once had a market; although trading ceased centuries ago, it is still possible to make out the shape of the Market Place.

NORTHREPPS
The Cottage and the Country Club c1955
Northrepps Cottage was built for Bartlett Gurney by Norwich architect William Wilkins in the 1790s. Anna Gurney, the translator of the 'Anglo-Saxon Chronicle', lived here for many years: she was paralysed and had to be carried down to the nearby beach that she loved.

◆

MELTON CONSTABLE
The Village c1955
In the late 19th century, Melton Constable was an important railway junction with locomotive and rolling stock works; it was sometimes known as the Crewe of Norfolk. Some of the streets of terraced houses built for railway workers still survive, but no trains have run here since 1965.

NORTHREPPS, THE COTTAGE AND THE COUNTRY CLUB C1965 N129003

MELTON CONSTABLE, THE VILLAGE C1955 M59009

MUNDESLEY, GENERAL VIEW c1955 M109005

Despite an attempt to develop the town as a seaside resort, Mundesley remains essentially a village. One of the attractions of this coast was the health-giving quality of the sea air. There were two sanitoria in Mundesley, one of which advertised revolving shelters for TB patients.

MUNDESLEY, KILN CLIFFS c1955 M109057

Two brick kilns were erected here in the 1890s to supply bricks for an intended new estate. The development never happened; one problem was the continual danger of erosion of the cliffs. This kiln is now surrounded by holiday caravans and chalets.

MUNDESLEY, THE PARADE c1965 M109064

This little group of shops was built in 1908, on the site of a former wheelwright and boat-building business. In the distance is the Manor House Hotel, the grandest in the town: in 1949 full board here cost no less than 42 shillings a day. It had its own private staircase down to the beach.

OVERSTRAND, MAIN STREET c1965 O31108

Overstrand developed as a resort slightly later than its neighbour Cromer. It has two large villas and a Methodist Chapel built by the well-known architect Sir Edwin Lutyens, most famous as the designer of the city of New Delhi. It has always been grander than Cromer, and is sometimes called 'The Village of Millionaires'.

CROMER
East Beach c1955 C192013
Cromer developed as a seaside resort in the early
19th century - it is mentioned as a bathing-place in
Jane Austen's 'Emma'. The Esplanade was laid out
in 1894. Cromer lighthouse is just
over the crest of the hill.

CROMER, THE PIER c1955 C192046

CROMER
The Pier c1955
Cromer Pier was built in 1900 and has offered
entertainment ever since. It is often advertised as
being the only place in England from which one
can watch the sun both rise and set over the sea.
The pier was damaged during World War Two, and
only reopened a few years before this
photograph was taken.

◆

CROMER
Church Street c1960
The parish church of St Peter and St Paul has the
tallest tower of any in Norfolk, rising to 160 feet.
The town developed after the railway reached it in
1877, and much more rapidly after the introduction
of through trains from London some ten years later.

CROMER, CHURCH STREET c1960 C192078

WEST RUNTON, THE VILLAGE c1955 W70070

The most famous inhabitant of West Runton died some 600,000 years ago: the skeleton of a giant elephant was found in the cliffs after erosion in the 1990s. It is the most complete such skeleton in the world, and is on display at Norwich Castle Museum.

WEST RUNTON, MAIN STREET c1955 W70084

There are a surprising number and variety of shops for such a small village, reflecting the need to cater not only for local inhabitants but also for campers and caravanners on the cliffs between the village and the sea.

EAST RUNTON, THE BEACH E11036

The concrete slipway is for fishing boats, which are dragged to the water by the tank-like vehicle. The beach is for pleasure too, with beach huts and deck chairs, both offered for hire by W Green and Son. Cromer pier can be seen in the distance.

EAST RUNTON, HIGH STREET c1955 E11019

This narrow road is still the main highway along the north Norfolk coast. The caravan site on the right is on top of the Runton cliffs. The sea is immediately to the right of the caravan park; there are steep steps down to the beach here, as at several other places on the Norfolk coast.

SHERINGHAM, CHURCH STREET c1955 S116037

Old - or Upper - Sheringham is on a hill well inland; the town only developed towards the sea in the late 19th and early 20th century. It never reached the size of Hunstanton or Cromer, and fishing is still as important as tourism here: crabs and lobsters are the main catches.

SHERINGHAM, WEST BEACH c1955 S116085

The north coast resorts have beaches of pebbles, unlike the sandy beaches of the east coast. The groynes run out to sea in an attempt to prevent the pebbles being pushed along the beach by the action of the waves. The esplanade also helps prevent the erosion of the cliff.

HOLT

High Street c1955 H102010

The postman carries an unsafe-looking load on his
bicycle. Holt has been a market town since the time
of Edward II; the town suffered a major fire in 1708.
Sir John Gresham founded the grammar school
here, still known as Gresham's School: old boys
include Sir John Reith, founder of the BBC.

WEYBOURNE, THE VILLAGE c1955 W353015
The village is dominated by the parish church with its 15th-century flint tower; it is surrounded by the ruins of the priory founded here in the time of King John by Sir Ralph Mainwaring. The church was shared by the canons and the parishioners.

SALTHOUSE, CROSS STREET c1955 S507017
This scene is characteristic of the North Norfolk coast: the walls and houses are built of whole flints found in the fields or on the nearby beach. Flint and brick used together can produce charming patterns, as we can see on the gable-end in the centre of this picture.

CLEY-NEXT-THE-SEA, THE VILLAGE c1955 C118004

Two of the buildings in this narrow main street are former inns: the one on the right, with its fine 19th-century shopfront, and the large building at the end of the street, which was built in the early 18th century.

CLEY-NEXT-THE-SEA, THE WINDMILL c1955 C118010

Pebble-built cottages line the coast road to the corn windmill, which stands immediately behind the 17th-century harbour. The mill was converted to holiday accommodation as early as 1921. The church in the distance is not Cley but Blakeney.

BLAKENEY
The Church c1960 B121016
The small tower at the far end of the church served as a mark for
sailors heading for the port: it used to carry a beacon at night.
Blakeney was a major port when this church was built,
its ships trading as far away as Iceland.

BLAKENEY, THE FERRY BOAT c1955 B121054
The 'Snow Goose' ferry leaves the Quay, still busy with fishing boats. The large building behind is the Blakeney Hotel, which opened in 1923. The area is visited for its bird-watching rather than its beaches.

GLANDFORD, THE FORD AND THE CHURCH c1965 G209161
Glandford village was built as a model village by Sir Alfred Jodrell of nearby Bayfield Hall in the late 19th century. He built the church too, reusing material from the derelict medieval church.

The North-West

MORSTON
THE VILLAGE c1955 M248064
Blakeney Point, a shingle peninsula owned by the National Trust, is a haven for wild birds and also the home of thousands of seals. These are best seen from boats boarded either at Blakeney or here at Morston, a mile further west.

WELLS-NEXT-THE-SEA
The Harbour c1955 W48066
Wells was a port long before it became a tourist
town, as the functional harbour and large
warehouses make clear. The parish register for 1583
records the loss of a Wells ship coming from Spain
on the west coast of England. Fourteen sailors were
drowned; the wreck was blamed on a curse laid on
the ship by a witch from Lynn.

WELLS-NEXT-THE-SEA, STAITHE STREET c1955 W48043
This is a narrow street of 18th- and 19th-century houses leading down to the harbour. The grid pattern of the streets in the centre of Wells strongly suggests that the town was a planned one, probably by the abbey of Ramsey (in Lincolnshire) which owned it some 700 years ago.

WELLS-NEXT-THE-SEA, THE QUAY c1965 W48113
We are looking out from Wells towards the sea. This photograph was taken at high tide, otherwise extensive mud flats would be visible. The woods on the left-hand side are part of the Holkham estate. Beyond the trees are sandy but dangerous beaches, where the tide comes in faster than a man can run.

HOLKHAM, THE VILLAGE STORES c1955 H340002

HOLKHAM
The Village Stores c1955
Cigarettes, films and ice cream are among the heavily advertised items stocked at the village stores. The village stands at the edge of the park of Holkham Hall, the palatial 18th-century home of Thomas Coke, later Earl of Leicester.

WALSINGHAM
The Gatehouse c1965
Walsingham Priory was visited by more pilgrims in the Middle Ages than any other site in England, apart from Canterbury. They came to see the Holy House, a miraculous re-creation of the house in Nazareth where Jesus was brought up, together with other wonders. Every medieval king of England came here, and would have entered the priory grounds through this gateway.

WALSINGHAM, THE GATEHOUSE c1965 W13053

WALSINGHAM, THE COMMON PLACE c1965 W13050

The town of Little Walsingham grew up to serve the many thousands of pilgrims that came to the priory; it has more early 17th-century houses than any other town in Norfolk. The water conduit is of the same date, and is surmounted by a beacon.

FAKENHAM, MARKET PLACE c1955 F3001

As a market town, Fakenham serves the needs of a wide area of villages and farms - as is suggested by the presence of the main national banks. The men in the foreground are probably from the United States Air Force base at nearby Sculthorpe.

FAKENHAM
NORWICH STREET c1955 F3002
Here we see the main street, with the sign of the Home and Colonial Stores prominent on the left and Universal Suppliers on the right. The postman pushes a large wicker-basket on wheels containing the day's letters and parcels.

BURNHAM OVERY, THE VILLAGE c1955 B819004

The name of this inn is the Hero, after the most famous inhabitant of the Burnhams: Horatio Nelson, born in the rectory of nearby Burnham Thorpe, and later to become England's greatest admiral, and victor of the Nile, Copenhagen, Trafalgar and other battles.

BURNHAM MARKET, EVERETTS MILL BRIDGE c1955 B500020

The Burnhams take their name from the river Burn, which runs through this picture. The mill and bridge were built in 1790, with warehouses being added to the right of the main building in the 19th century.

NORTH CREAKE, THE BRIDGE c1960 N138005

NORTH CREAKE
The Bridge c1960

The river Burn runs through the villages of South and North Creake too. The road at the centre of the picture leads to the ruins of Creake Abbey, which lies in a beautiful setting beside the stream. The abbey came to a sudden end in 1506 when all its occupants died of plague within a week.

◆

BRANCASTER
St Mary's Church c1965

The parish church is of flint, with a large west tower. A tombstone in the churchyard records the burial of Alexander and Susan Roche, two of eleven people drowned when the 'Earl of Wemyss' ran aground here in a gale in August 1833. The inscription on the stone says that unscrupulous thieves plundered the bodies as they lay on the beach.

BRANCASTER, ST MARY'S CHURCH c1965 B401007

OLD HUNSTANTON, THE CHURCH c1955 O119103

The parish church of St Mary is here seen under scaffolding. The tower is 15th-century, but most of the remainder of the building was rebuilt in the 1850s. The interior has many interesting monuments to the L'Estrange family, who owned nearby Hunstanton Hall. The writer P G Wodehouse was a friend of the family and a frequent visitor to the Hall.

HUNSTANTON, DONKEY RIDES c1955 H135060

Hunstanton, with its sandy beach, is the most popular seaside town in north-west Norfolk. It is famous for its cliffs, which are made up of three differently-coloured rocks in horizontal bands - white, red and orange-brown.

HUNSTANTON
The Artificial Rowing Lake c1965

In the 20th century, Hunstanton has spread southwards from its Victorian centre, offering entertainments such as the Blue Lagoon Swimming Pool, opened in 1927, and this Boating Lake, opened in 1932.

INGOLDISTHORPE
The Village c1965

Ingoldisthorpe is an open village on the sandy soils of north-west Norfolk. When Eleanor Tylden celebrated her 100th birthday here in 1923, she was visited by no less than three queens - Queen Alexandra, Queen Mary and Queen Maud of Norway, all from the nearby royal estate at Sandringham.

HUNSTANTON, THE ARTIFICIAL ROWING LAKE c1965 H135119

INGOLDISTHORPE, THE VILLAGE c1965 I45025

HEACHAM, THE VILLAGE GREEN c1965 H57103

The archway on the left led to Heacham Hall. John Rolfe of the Hall married the Indian princess Pocahontas in Jamestown, Virginia in 1614, and brought her back to England. She is supposed to have lived with him here at Heacham, before sickening for her home in America. She died at Gravesend on the long journey home.

HEACHAM, SOUTH BEACH c1965 H57116

The line of beach-huts makes a striking background to this picture of a father and son sea fishing from the pebbly beach. The peaceful sea could be deceptive: a memorial in the church relates to nine local people who went boating one Sunday in 1799 and never came back.

SNETTISHAM
The Village Sign c1960

The circular object at the top of the sign represents a torc or neck ornament. A fabulous collection of more than a hundred gold, silver and electrum torcs, dating from the Iron Age, was found here: they are now in Norwich Castle Museum.

SNETTISHAM
The Village c1960

Snettisham has a fascinating church with a west front modelled on that of Peterborough Cathedral and one of the few medieval stone spires in Norfolk. The churchyard was the setting for the Snettisham Ghost, a late Victorian apparition described by the writer Andrew Lang and others.

SNETTISHAM, THE VILLAGE SIGN c1960 S464022

SNETTISHAM, THE VILLAGE c1960 S464007

GREAT BIRCHAM
The Country Stores c1960
This shop frontage shows the development of the village shop into the mini-supermarket, ultra-modern for its time. A hundred years earlier there had been no less than four shops in this village, and a bakery as well.

◆

DERSINGHAM
Hunstanton Road c1965
Dersingham is on the ridge running north towards Hunstanton; many of the houses are built of local carstone. Almost all the land in the village is part of the 20,000 acre Sandringham estate owned by the Queen.

GREAT BIRCHAM, THE COUNTRY STORES c1960 G190038

DERSINGHAM, HUNSTANTON ROAD c1965 D148014

SANDRINGHAM
The House from the Lake c1955

Sandringham has been a royal palace since 1861, when Prince Albert purchased the estate to give his son, the Prince of Wales, a country estate with good shooting, well away from the temptations of London.

◆

WOLFERTON
The Station c1955

One of the earliest railway stations in England, Wolferton has a suite of royal waiting rooms that were used by the Prince of Wales and his friends. The rooms were built in 1876 and extended in 1898 to provide separate rooms for the Prince and for his wife Princess Alexandra.

SANDRINGHAM, THE HOUSE FROM THE LAKE c1955 S58029

WOLFERTON, THE STATION c1955 W354002

CASTLE RISING, TRINITY HOSPITAL c1960 C45016
The Hospital was founded by Henry Howard, Earl of Northampton, in the early 17th century. The old ladies in the hospital were given a uniform of red cloaks and steeple hats, which may still occasionally be seen in the town.

GAYWOOD, THE CLOCK TOWER c1965 G189020
The Clock Tower is an uncommon form of memorial to the fallen of World War I: it was first erected in 1920, and has since been moved slightly to avoid obstructing the traffic. Once a village in its own right, Gaywood had become no more than a suburb of Lynn by the date of this photograph.

KING'S LYNN, TUESDAY MARKET PLACE c1955 K28016
Lynn has two market places, holding markets on different days of the week. The large stone building is the Corn Exchange, built in 1854: Ceres, the goddess of plenty, stands at the top. The town pillory stood in this Market Place, and a pleasure fair was also held here.

KING'S LYNN, SATURDAY MARKET PLACE AND THE GUILDHALL c1955 K28025
The Guildhall is the building with the large window: it was built in 1422-1428. To the immediate right is the borough gaol of 1784. Lynn was founded by Herbert, Bishop of Norwich, in about 1100; it was known as Bishop's Lynn until it passed to the Crown in the time of Henry VIII.

CLENCHWARTON, THE SCHOOL c1965 C416015
This is a good example of a Board School. These were set up in the 1870s to provide education in places where no schools had been established by religious bodies. Boys and girls usually had in effect separate schools in one building, each with its own entrance.

South-West Norfolk

OUTWELL
High Street c1965 O79016
Outwell and Upwell together make up one large
village running for four miles along the old course of
the river Nene. There was an early tramway here,
connecting the villages with Wisbech: it opened in
1882, but closed to passengers in 1929.

STOWBRIDGE, THE RIVER AND THE BRIDGE c1965 S689006

The river Ouse has always formed a major barrier to traffic heading into Norfolk from the west. The two main crossings were here, at Stow Bardolph, and at nearby Magdalen bridge: these were droving roads used by cattle traders, and there was formerly a major cattle fair here at Stow.

DOWNHAM MARKET, MARKET PLACE c1955 D149041

The unusual Gothic-style clock tower was built in 1878 by William Cunliffe: it is made of cast-iron. Horatio Nelson was at school in Downham Market in the later 18th century; a fellow-pupil was George Manby, inventor of the life-saving rocket.

DOWNHAM MARKET, DENVER SLUICE c1965 D149005

The whole area of the Fens is largely below sea level, and is dependent on a system of channels and sluices for protection against flooding. The lock was built by Sir James Rennie in 1834 to replace a less massive structure that had given way under the pressure of the water.

TEN MILE BANK, THE VILLAGE c1955 T225005

The village's name derives from a long bank along the river Ouse, on the right of the photograph, defending the low-lying land from flooding. The building at the end of the row of houses is a Primitive Methodist chapel.

WEST DEREHAM, CHURCH ROAD c1955 W338004
The round tower of the parish church can be seen in the distance. West Dereham was the birthplace of Hubert
Walter, who was a friend and fellow-crusader of Richard the Lionheart; he later became Archbishop of Canterbury.
He founded an abbey in his home village, parts of which survive in Abbey Farm.

WEST DEREHAM
The Chequers and the Post Office c1955
W338012

The inn and the post office (and general stores) were at the heart of most villages until very recent times. There was a weekly market here, granted to the abbey by King John in 1199: it had fallen out of use by the 16th century. The isolation of this area of Norfolk is shown by the fact that the local railway station was closed to passenger traffic as early as 1930.

NARBOROUGH
THE VILLAGE c1955 N189019
This is one of several villages in west Norfolk where the main building material is local carstone, rather than the flint used throughout the rest of the county: the buildings to the left of the photograph are good examples. Narborough straddles the river Nar and has two watermills.

METHWOLD, THE GEORGE INN c1960 M229009

The church, like the inn, is dedicated to St George: with its lantern tower and steeple rising to 120 feet, it is visible for miles around in this flat landscape. Methwold is one of several south-west Norfolk parishes noted for rabbit farming: there was an enormous warren here, covering 1,500 acres.

CASTLE ACRE, BAILEY GATE c1955 C41032

This town contains as many historic features as any small town in England. It has a large Norman Castle, and extensive remains of a medieval Cluniac priory. There was a medieval planned town running between the two: this early 13th-century gate is its northern entrance.

SWAFFHAM
Market Place c1955 S237002

Here we see the large triangular market place, with the
parish church beyond. Tradition says that the church was
built largely at the expense of the 'Swaffham pedlar' - one
John Chapman, who was lucky enough to find two pots of
gold in his garden after being guided to them in a dream.

◆

WATTON, THE TOWN SIGN AND THE CLOCK TOWER c1955 W383015
The clock tower dates from 1679. The coat of arms of Watton is a hare and a barrel: they can be seen above the clock and again on the weather vane. ('Wat' is a dialect word for a hare, and 'tun' a word for a barrel.) Near Watton is Wayland Wood, the traditional site of the original murders behind the pantomime story of the Babes in the Wood.

THETFORD
Haling Path c1955 T31006
The Haling Path, from which this picture is taken, is the
path along the river used by horses pulling barges. The
bridge is the Thetford Town Bridge, a cast-iron structure
that dates from 1829. Thomas Paine, the author of 'The
Rights of Man' and participant in both the American
and French revolutions, was born in Thetford in 1737.

◆

Central and South-East Norfolk

EAST DEREHAM
CHURCH STREET c1955 D25010
The tower dominating this picture is the bell-tower, built in 1515-1525; an equally massive church tower is hidden behind the tree. In the early 19th century, the bell-tower was used to house French prisoners of war: one, shot while trying to escape, is buried in the adjoining churchyard.

EAST DEREHAM, THE TOWN SIGN c1954 D25100

This sign commemorates St Withburga, a Saxon princess, who supposedly founded a monastery here in the year 654. She was provided with milk by two deer; when a huntsman came after them with dogs, he was struck down by God and died instantly.

HINGHAM, THE MARKET PLACE c1955 H309011

Hingham was an important market town in the Middle Ages. It will always be associated with the Lincoln family, as the ancestors of President Abraham Lincoln lived here for many generations and are commemorated by a bust of the President in the parish church.

GREAT ELLINGHAM, THE MILL c1960 G191010

The tower of the corn windmill dominates the picture despite having lost its sails and cap. The road from Great Ellingham to Hingham runs dead straight for over half a mile, an unusual survival of an open-field boundary from the Middle Ages.

EAST HARLING, THE SQUARE c1965 E132012

Shops and private houses of all dates surround the large Market Square. In the 19th century, locally-made wool and hemp products were being sold here, and dairy products were sold on the appropriately-named Cheese Hill. East Harling church contains some very fine monuments to local families and the best medieval glass in Norfolk.

BANHAM, THE GREEN C1965 B494012
Here we see an exceptionally pretty village green, lined on all sides with trees. The War Memorial now dominates the green: according to the Norfolk Roll of Honour, 39 men from this little village were killed in World War I.

GARBOLDISHAM, CHURCH ROAD C1955 G188003
Garboldisham is steeped in ancient history: there is a defensive earth work here known as the Devil's Dyke, and a mound traditionally supposed to be the grave of Boudicca, Queen of the Iceni. It is difficult to imagine that this peaceful village was a market town in the Middle Ages.

DISS, MARKET HILL C1965 D32019

Early closing day gives a peaceful air to this normally busy market town, built around a six-acre lake known as Diss Mere: local tradition says that it is bottomless. John Skelton, poet laureate and tutor to Henry VIII, was born here and served as rector for 25 years.

SCOLE, THE VILLAGE C1955 S508002

Scole is on the old main road south from Norwich. The large coaching-inn is the White Hart, which once boasted perhaps the most famous inn sign in England, an enormous wooden structure stretching right across the street which included 25 life-size figures.

HARLESTON
The Thoroughfare c1955 H305005
The Georgian coaching-inn, the Swan Hotel,
dominates the street. The clock tower was built
in 1873 to replace a church on the site, which
had itself been replaced by a new church
in nearby Broad Street.

HARLESTON, THE MARKET PLACE c1955 H305002

The market here was established under a royal charter of 1372; by the 19th century it was specialising in lambs and cattle. The Magpie Hotel, with its fine inn sign, was built in about 1710.

LONG STRATTON, THE VILLAGE c1965 L300001

The name means simply 'long street', and the village is spread along the main road, originally the Roman road running from London to Caistor St Edmund, the Roman town just south of Norwich.

LODDON, THE OLD SCHOOL C1965 L369017

This is a Gothic-style school built by the innovative architect J S Benest in 1857 and extended in 1881. The nearby parish church includes a rare painting of Sir John Hobart kneeling before Henry VII, with a picture of Loddon church as the background.

BRAMERTON, THE VILLAGE 1953 B301004

This small south Norfolk village runs along a single street. The high pitch of the roof on the house to the right suggests that it may originally have been of thatch. There is a riverside inn at Bramerton called the Wood's End: its recorded history stretches back well over 300 years.

Index

Frith Book Co Titles

www.francisfrith.co.uk

The Frith Book Company publishes over 100 new titles each year. A selection of those currently available are listed below. For latest catalogue please contact Frith Book Co.

Town Books 96 pages, approx 100 photos. County and Themed Books 128 pages, approx 150 photos (unless specified). All titles hardback laminated case and jacket except those indicated pb (paperback)

Title	ISBN	Price	Title	ISBN	Price
Amersham, Chesham & Rickmansworth (pb)			Derby (pb)	1-85937-367-4	£9.99
	1-85937-340-2	£9.99	Derbyshire (pb)	1-85937-196-5	£9.99
Ancient Monuments & Stone Circles	1-85937-143-4	£17.99	Devon (pb)	1-85937-297-x	£9.99
Aylesbury (pb)	1-85937-227-9	£9.99	Dorset (pb)	1-85937-269-4	£9.99
Bakewell	1-85937-113-2	£12.99	Dorset Churches	1-85937-172-8	£17.99
Barnstaple (pb)	1-85937-300-3	£9.99	Dorset Coast (pb)	1-85937-299-6	£9.99
Bath (pb)	1-85937-419-0	£9.99	Dorset Living Memories	1-85937-210-4	£14.99
Bedford (pb)	1-85937-205-8	£9.99	Down the Severn	1-85937-118-3	£14.99
Berkshire (pb)	1-85937-191-4	£9.99	Down the Thames (pb)	1-85937-278-3	£9.99
Berkshire Churches	1-85937-170-1	£17.99	Down the Trent	1-85937-311-9	£14.99
Blackpool (pb)	1-85937-382-8	£9.99	Dublin (pb)	1-85937-231-7	£9.99
Bognor Regis (pb)	1-85937-431-x	£9.99	East Anglia (pb)	1-85937-265-1	£9.99
Bournemouth	1-85937-067-5	£12.99	East London	1-85937-080-2	£14.99
Bradford (pb)	1-85937-204-x	£9.99	East Sussex	1-85937-130-2	£14.99
Brighton & Hove(pb)	1-85937-192-2	£8.99	Eastbourne	1-85937-061-6	£12.99
Bristol (pb)	1-85937-264-3	£9.99	Edinburgh (pb)	1-85937-193-0	£8.99
British Life A Century Ago (pb)	1-85937-213-9	£9.99	England in the 1880s	1-85937-331-3	£17.99
Buckinghamshire (pb)	1-85937-200-7	£9.99	English Castles (pb)	1-85937-434-4	£9.99
Camberley (pb)	1-85937-222-8	£9.99	English Country Houses	1-85937-161-2	£17.99
Cambridge (pb)	1-85937-422-0	£9.99	Essex (pb)	1-85937-270-8	£9.99
Cambridgeshire (pb)	1-85937-420-4	£9.99	Exeter	1-85937-126-4	£12.99
Canals & Waterways (pb)	1-85937-291-0	£9.99	Exmoor	1-85937-132-9	£14.99
Canterbury Cathedral (pb)	1-85937-179-5	£9.99	Falmouth	1-85937-066-7	£12.99
Cardiff (pb)	1-85937-093-4	£9.99	Folkestone (pb)	1-85937-124-8	£9.99
Carmarthenshire	1-85937-216-3	£14.99	Glasgow (pb)	1-85937-190-6	£9.99
Chelmsford (pb)	1-85937-310-0	£9.99	Gloucestershire	1-85937-102-7	£14.99
Cheltenham (pb)	1-85937-095-0	£9.99	Great Yarmouth (pb)	1-85937-426-3	£9.99
Cheshire (pb)	1-85937-271-6	£9.99	Greater Manchester (pb)	1-85937-266-x	£9.99
Chester	1-85937-090-x	£12.99	Guildford (pb)	1-85937-410-7	£9.99
Chesterfield	1-85937-378-x	£9.99	Hampshire (pb)	1-85937-279-1	£9.99
Chichester (pb)	1-85937-228-7	£9.99	Hampshire Churches (pb)	1-85937-207-4	£9.99
Colchester (pb)	1-85937-188-4	£8.99	Harrogate	1-85937-423-9	£9.99
Cornish Coast	1-85937-163-9	£14.99	Hastings & Bexhill (pb)	1-85937-131-0	£9.99
Cornwall (pb)	1-85937-229-5	£9.99	Heart of Lancashire (pb)	1-85937-197-3	£9.99
Cornwall Living Memories	1-85937-248-1	£14.99	Helston (pb)	1-85937-214-7	£9.99
Cotswolds (pb)	1-85937-230-9	£9.99	Hereford (pb)	1-85937-175-2	£9.99
Cotswolds Living Memories	1-85937-255-4	£14.99	Herefordshire	1-85937-174-4	£14.99
County Durham	1-85937-123-x	£14.99	Hertfordshire (pb)	1-85937-247-3	£9.99
Croydon Living Memories	1-85937-162-0	£9.99	Horsham (pb)	1-85937-432-8	£9.99
Cumbria	1-85937-101-9	£14.99	Humberside	1-85937-215-5	£14.99
Dartmoor	1-85937-145-0	£14.99	Hythe, Romney Marsh & Ashford	1-85937-256-2	£9.99

Available from your local bookshop or from the publisher

Frith Book Co Titles (continued)

Title	ISBN	Price		Title	ISBN	Price
Ipswich (pb)	1-85937-424-7	£9.99		St Ives (pb)	1-85937415-8	£9.99
Ireland (pb)	1-85937-181-7	£9.99		Scotland (pb)	1-85937-182-5	£9.99
Isle of Man (pb)	1-85937-268-6	£9.99		Scottish Castles (pb)	1-85937-323-2	£9.99
Isles of Scilly	1-85937-136-1	£14.99		Sevenoaks & Tunbridge	1-85937-057-8	£12.99
Isle of Wight (pb)	1-85937-429-8	£9.99		Sheffield, South Yorks (pb)	1-85937-267-8	£9.99
Isle of Wight Living Memories	1-85937-304-6	£14.99		Shrewsbury (pb)	1-85937-325-9	£9.99
Kent (pb)	1-85937-189-2	£9.99		Shropshire (pb)	1-85937-326-7	£9.99
Kent Living Memories	1-85937-125-6	£14.99		Somerset	1-85937-153-1	£14.99
Lake District (pb)	1-85937-275-9	£9.99		South Devon Coast	1-85937-107-8	£14.99
Lancaster, Morecambe & Heysham (pb)	1-85937-233-3	£9.99		South Devon Living Memories	1-85937-168-x	£14.99
Leeds (pb)	1-85937-202-3	£9.99		South Hams	1-85937-220-1	£14.99
Leicester	1-85937-073-x	£12.99		Southampton (pb)	1-85937-427-1	£9.99
Leicestershire (pb)	1-85937-185-x	£9.99		Southport (pb)	1-85937-425-5	£9.99
Lincolnshire (pb)	1-85937-433-6	£9.99		Staffordshire	1-85937-047-0	£12.99
Liverpool & Merseyside (pb)	1-85937-234-1	£9.99		Stratford upon Avon	1-85937-098-5	£12.99
London (pb)	1-85937-183-3	£9.99		Suffolk (pb)	1-85937-221-x	£9.99
Ludlow (pb)	1-85937-176-0	£9.99		Suffolk Coast	1-85937-259-7	£14.99
Luton (pb)	1-85937-235-x	£9.99		Surrey (pb)	1-85937-240-6	£9.99
Maidstone	1-85937-056-x	£14.99		Sussex (pb)	1-85937-184-1	£9.99
Manchester (pb)	1-85937-198-1	£9.99		Swansea (pb)	1-85937-167-1	£9.99
Middlesex	1-85937-158-2	£14.99		Tees Valley & Cleveland	1-85937-211-2	£14.99
New Forest	1-85937-128-0	£14.99		Thanet (pb)	1-85937-116-7	£9.99
Newark (pb)	1-85937-366-6	£9.99		Tiverton (pb)	1-85937-178-7	£9.99
Newport, Wales (pb)	1-85937-258-9	£9.99		Torbay	1-85937-063-2	£12.99
Newquay (pb)	1-85937-421-2	£9.99		Truro	1-85937-147-7	£12.99
Norfolk (pb)	1-85937-195-7	£9.99		Victorian and Edwardian Cornwall	1-85937-252-x	£14.99
Norfolk Living Memories	1-85937-217-1	£14.99		Victorian & Edwardian Devon	1-85937-253-8	£14.99
Northamptonshire	1-85937-150-7	£14.99		Victorian & Edwardian Kent	1-85937-149-3	£14.99
Northumberland Tyne & Wear (pb)	1-85937-281-3	£9.99		Vic & Ed Maritime Album	1-85937-144-2	£17.99
North Devon Coast	1-85937-146-9	£14.99		Victorian and Edwardian Sussex	1-85937-157-4	£14.99
North Devon Living Memories	1-85937-261-9	£14.99		Victorian & Edwardian Yorkshire	1-85937-154-x	£14.99
North London	1-85937-206-6	£14.99		Victorian Seaside	1-85937-159-0	£17.99
North Wales (pb)	1-85937-298-8	£9.99		Villages of Devon (pb)	1-85937-293-7	£9.99
North Yorkshire (pb)	1-85937-236-8	£9.99		Villages of Kent (pb)	1-85937-294-5	£9.99
Norwich (pb)	1-85937-194-9	£8.99		Villages of Sussex (pb)	1-85937-295-3	£9.99
Nottingham (pb)	1-85937-324-0	£9.99		Warwickshire (pb)	1-85937-203-1	£9.99
Nottinghamshire (pb)	1-85937-187-6	£9.99		Welsh Castles (pb)	1-85937-322-4	£9.99
Oxford (pb)	1-85937-411-5	£9.99		West Midlands (pb)	1-85937-289-9	£9.99
Oxfordshire (pb)	1-85937-430-1	£9.99		West Sussex	1-85937-148-5	£14.99
Peak District (pb)	1-85937-280-5	£9.99		West Yorkshire (pb)	1-85937-201-5	£9.99
Penzance	1-85937-069-1	£12.99		Weymouth (pb)	1-85937-209-0	£9.99
Peterborough (pb)	1-85937-219-8	£9.99		Wiltshire (pb)	1-85937-277-5	£9.99
Piers	1-85937-237-6	£17.99		Wiltshire Churches (pb)	1-85937-171-x	£9.99
Plymouth	1-85937-119-1	£12.99		Wiltshire Living Memories	1-85937-245-7	£14.99
Poole & Sandbanks (pb)	1-85937-251-1	£9.99		Winchester (pb)	1-85937-428-x	£9.99
Preston (pb)	1-85937-212-0	£9.99		Windmills & Watermills	1-85937-242-2	£17.99
Reading (pb)	1-85937-238-4	£9.99		Worcester (pb)	1-85937-165-5	£9.99
Romford (pb)	1-85937-319-4	£9.99		Worcestershire	1-85937-152-3	£14.99
Salisbury (pb)	1-85937-239-2	£9.99		York (pb)	1-85937-199-x	£9.99
Scarborough (pb)	1-85937-379-8	£9.99		Yorkshire (pb)	1-85937-186-8	£9.99
St Albans (pb)	1-85937-341-0	£9.99		Yorkshire Living Memories	1-85937-166-3	£14.99

See Frith books on the internet www.francisfrith.co.uk

FRITH PRODUCTS & SERVICES

Francis Frith would doubtless be pleased to know that the pioneering publishing venture he started in 1860 still continues today. A hundred and forty years later, The Francis Frith Collection continues in the same innovative tradition and is now one of the foremost publishers of vintage photographs in the world. Some of the current activities include:

Interior Decoration

Today Frith's photographs can be seen framed and as giant wall murals in thousands of pubs, restaurants, hotels, banks, retail stores and other public buildings throughout the country. In every case they enhance the unique local atmosphere of the places they depict and provide reminders of gentler days in an increasingly busy and frenetic world.

Product Promotions

Frith products are used by many major companies to promote the sales of their own products or to reinforce their own history and heritage. Frith promotions have been used by Hovis bread, Courage beers, Scots Porage Oats, Colman's mustard, Cadbury's foods, Mellow Birds coffee, Dunhill pipe tobacco, Guinness, and Bulmer's Cider.

Genealogy and Family History

As the interest in family history and roots grows world-wide, more and more people are turning to Frith's photographs of Great Britain for images of the towns, villages and streets where their ancestors lived; and, of course, photographs of the churches and chapels where their ancestors were christened, married and buried are an essential part of every genealogy tree and family album.

Frith Products

All Frith photographs are available Framed or just as Mounted Prints and Posters (size 23 x 16 inches). These may be ordered from the address below. From time to time other products - Address Books, Calendars, Table Mats, etc - are available.

The Internet

Already twenty thousand Frith photographs can be viewed and purchased on the internet through the Frith websites and a myriad of partner sites.

For more detailed information on Frith companies and products, look at these sites:

www.francisfrith.co.uk
www.francisfrith.com
(for North American visitors)

See the complete list of Frith Books at:
www.francisfrith.co.uk
This web site is regularly updated with the latest list of publications from the Frith Book Company. If you wish to buy books relating to another part of the country that your local bookshop does not stock, you may purchase on-line.

For further information, trade, or author enquiries please contact us at the address below:
The Francis Frith Collection, Frith's Barn, Teffont, Salisbury, Wiltshire, England SP3 5QP.
Tel: +44 (0)1722 716 376 Fax: +44 (0)1722 716 881   Email: sales@francisfrith.co.uk

See Frith books on the internet www.francisfrith.co.uk

TO RECEIVE YOUR **FREE** MOUNTED PRINT

Mounted Print
Overall size 14 x 11 inches

Cut out this Voucher and return it with your remittance for £1.95 to cover postage and handling, to UK addresses. For overseas addresses please include £4.00 post and handling. Choose any photograph included in this book. Your SEPIA print will be A4 in size, and mounted in a cream mount with burgundy rule line, overall size 14 x 11 inches.

Order additional Mounted Prints at HALF PRICE (only £7.49 each*)

If there are further pictures you would like to order, possibly as gifts for friends and family, purchase them at half price (no additional postage and handling required).

Have your Mounted Prints framed*

For an additional £14.95 per print you can have your chosen Mounted Print framed in an elegant polished wood and gilt moulding, overall size 16 x 13 inches (no additional postage and handling required).

---

* IMPORTANT!
These special prices are only available if ordered using the original voucher on this page (no copies permitted) and at the same time as your free Mounted Print, for delivery to the same address

---

Frith Collectors' Guild

From time to time we publish a magazine of news and stories about Frith photographs and further special offers of Frith products. If you would like 12 months FREE membership, please return this form.

Send completed forms to:
The Francis Frith Collection, Frith's Barn, Teffont, Salisbury, Wiltshire SP3 5QP

Voucher for **FREE** and Reduced Price Frith Prints

Picture no.	Page number	Qty	Mounted @ £7.49	Framed + £14.95	Total Cost
		1	**Free of charge***	£	£
			£7.49	£	£
			£7.49	£	£
			£7.49	£	£
			£7.49	£	£
			£7.49	£	£

Please allow 28 days for delivery	*** Post & handling**	**£1.95**
Book Title	**Total Order Cost**	**£**

Please do not photocopy this voucher. Only the original is valid, so please cut it out and return it to us.

I enclose a cheque / postal order for £ . . . .
made payable to 'The Francis Frith Collection'
OR please debit my Mastercard / Visa / Switch / Amex card
(credit cards please on all overseas orders)

Number . . . .

Issue No(Switch only) . . . . .Valid from (Amex/Switch) . . . .

Expires . . . . Signature . . . .

Name Mr/Mrs/Ms . . . .

Address . . . .

. . . .

. . . .

. . . . Postcode . . . .

Daytime Tel No . . . .   Valid to 31/12/02

The Francis Frith Collectors' Guild
Please enrol me as a member for 12 months free of charge.

Name Mr/Mrs/Ms . . . .

Address . . . .

. . . .

. . . .

. . . . Postcode . . . .

Would you like to find out more about Francis Frith?

We have recently recruited some entertaining speakers who are happy to visit local groups, clubs and societies to give an illustrated talk documenting Frith's travels and photographs. If you are a member of such a group and are interested in hosting a presentation, we would love to hear from you.

Our speakers bring with them a small selection of our local town and county books, together with sample prints. They are happy to take orders. A small proportion of the order value is donated to the group who have hosted the presentation. The talks are therefore an excellent way of fundraising for small groups and societies.

Can you help us with information about any of the Frith photographs in this book?

We are gradually compiling an historical record for each of the photographs in the Frith archive. It is always fascinating to find out the names of the people shown in the pictures, as well as insights into the shops, buildings and other features depicted.

If you recognize anyone in the photographs in this book, or if you have information not already included in the author's caption, do let us know. We would love to hear from you, and will try to publish it in future books or articles.

Our production team

Frith books are produced by a small dedicated team at offices in the converted Grade II listed 18th-century barn at Teffont near Salisbury, illustrated above. Most have worked with the Frith Collection for many years. All have in common one quality: they have a passion for the Frith Collection. The team is constantly expanding, but currently includes:

Jason Buck, John Buck, Douglas Burns, Heather Crisp, Isobel Hall, Rob Hames, Hazel Heaton, Peter Horne, James Kinnear, Tina Leary, Hannah Marsh, Eliza Sackett, Terence Sackett, Sandra Sanger, Shelley Tolcher, Susanna Walker, Clive Wathen and Jenny Wathen.